Blue Jeans

BEFORE THE STORE

BY JODY JENSEN SHAFFER • ILLUSTRATED BY DAN McGEEHAN

Published by The Child's World®
1980 Lookout Drive • Mankato, MN 56003-1705
800-599-READ • www.childsworld.com

ACKNOWLEDGMENTS
The Child's World®: Mary Berendes, Publishing Director
The Design Lab: Design and production
Red Line Editorial: Editorial direction
Content Consultant: S. Jack Hu, Ph.D., J. Reid and Polly Anderson Professor of Manufacturing Technology, Professor of Mechanical Engineering and Industrial and Operations Engineering, The University of Michigan

ISBN 9781609736286
LCCN 2011940070

PHOTO CREDITS
Baloncici/Dreamstime, cover, 1; Softdreams/Dreamstime, cover (inset), 1 (inset); iStockphoto, 5; Javier Soto Vazquez/Bigstock, 7; Linda Johnsonbaugh/Shutterstock Images, 9, 14, 30 (top left); Shutterstock Images, 11, 27, 31 (bottom left); Moreno Soppelsa/Shutterstock Images, 17, 19, 23, 31 (top left); Cross Design/Fotolia, 25, 30 (bottom left); Robert Peek/iStockphoto, 26, 30 (bottom right); Paul Prescott/Bigstock, 29, 31 (bottom right)

Design elements: Baloncici/Dreamstime

Printed in the United States of America

ABOUT THE AUTHOR

Jody Jensen Shaffer has taught college students and three year-olds. She writes for children from the home she shares with her husband, two kids, and dog in Missouri.

Contents

CHAPTER **1** **A Blue Jeans Day**   **4**

CHAPTER **2** **On the Cotton Farm**   **6**

CHAPTER **3** **Ginning Cotton**   **12**

CHAPTER **4** **At a Textile Mill**   **16**

CHAPTER **5** **At a Blue Jeans Factory**   **22**

CHAPTER **6** **Into Your Closet**   **28**

Blue Jeans Map, 30

Glossary, 32

Books and Web Sites, 32

Index, 32

CHAPTER ONE

A Blue Jeans Day

It is a cool fall day. You want to play outside. You grab a sweatshirt and your favorite pair of blue jeans. They feel soft and warm. They are strong. They are just the right shade of blue.

Have you thought about how blue jeans are made? There are many steps in the process. The first step starts at a cotton farm. That is where cotton plants are grown. Thread is made from cotton. It is an important part of blue jeans! Weaving thread makes blue jeans fabric. This fabric is called **denim**.

Everyone loves a pair of comfortable blue jeans.

CHAPTER TWO

On the Cotton Farm

Cotton is a **fiber** that grows on a plant. Farmers grow cotton plants on farms. Cotton plants use a lot of water to grow. They thrive in the sun. Cotton plants do not grow well in the cold.

Between February and June, farmers plant cottonseeds using tractors. One to two weeks after planting, small seedlings begin to show. Most cotton grows with the help of rain. Some farmers have to water their cotton if the land is dry.

Clothes and paper money are made from cotton fiber.

Cotton plants need lots of sunshine.

Farmers may spray cotton plants with **chemicals** to get rid of insects and pests. A beetle called a boll weevil can destroy cotton crops.

Around ten weeks after the cottonseeds are planted, flowers bloom on the plants. The blooms are cream colored. Then they turn pink and red before falling off.

Green buds take the place of the flowers. These buds look like small footballs. They are called cotton bolls or seed pods. Many cottonseeds are inside a cotton boll.

White fibers grow inside the cotton boll. Eight weeks after the cotton boll appears, it opens. The fiber is white and soft. The fibers dry in the warm air. This fluffs them up. Before farmers **harvest** cotton, they remove the leaves from the plants. This keeps the cotton white.

Machine pickers pick cotton quickly.

Farmers harvest cotton either by hand or with a machine called a picker. A picker pulls the cotton fibers from the plant. A different kind of machine, called a stripper, pulls the whole plant from the ground. One machine picker does the work of 50 people picking cotton by hand! Some cotton grows quickly. Some cotton grows slowly. Not all cotton can be picked at the same time. Two or three pickings may take place.

Once the cotton is picked it must be stored. It is pressed into large rectangles, similar to hay bales. The rectangles are called **modules**. Farmers cover the

modules with tarps to keep out the rain. When the
farmers are ready to take the modules to a cotton gin,
they load the modules onto a large truck.

Raw cotton is pressed into modules.

CHAPTER THREE

Ginning Cotton

A cotton gin is a machine used to separate cottonseeds from cotton. "Gin" is short for "engine." At a cotton gin, the cotton goes from modules into tubes. The tubes carry the cotton to a dryer. The dryer dries the cotton. Then machines clean the cotton. Sticks, leaves, and dirt are removed. The cotton is ready to be ginned.

Eli Whitney invented the cotton gin in 1793. Whitney's invention was very important for the United States. It helped the cotton industry grow quickly.

There are two ways to gin cotton. A saw gin grips short fibers. It pulls the cotton through thin slots. The cottonseeds are too big to pass through the slots.

A cotton gin removes seeds from cotton.

Cotton fabric is the most widely used fabric in the world.

A roller gin is used for long fibers. Roller gins do not hurt long fibers. They pull the fibers under a bar. The space below the bar is too small for seeds to pass through.

The cleaned fiber is now called lint. It is ready to be pressed into large bundles called bales. One bale

A machine presses lint into bales.

of cotton weighs about 500 pounds (227 kg). That is the weight of a baby elephant!

A worker uses a machine that lifts and moves cotton bales. The machine lifts the bales into trucks. The bales are shipped to **textile mills**, warehouses, and other countries.

After the cottonseeds have been separated from the cotton fibers, the seeds are stored. Then they are loaded onto trucks and taken to a cottonseed oil mill. Cottonseed oil is used to make crackers, cookies, and chips. Cottonseeds are also used to feed animals. Some cottonseeds are saved. They will be planted the next year.

CHAPTER FOUR

At a Textile Mill

A textile mill buys cotton lint. It makes yarn or cloth from it. There are many steps in making cloth from cotton.

First the cotton bales are opened. A machine pulls fibers from many bales. It mixes the cotton together with a mixing machine. Then the fibers are carded, or brushed.

A carding machine uses rollers with teeth to brush the lint. The lint is brushed into a soft, straight rope. This rope is called a sliver.

The cotton is pulled into long rope fibers called slivers.

The sliver is pulled and twisted to make it strong. Now the sliver is wound around a bobbin. Bobbins are used to store thread until it is ready to be spun. The thread can be woven or knitted into cloth.

Cotton thread is woven on a loom. A loom is a machine that weaves together two sets of yarn. Warp yarns go up and down. They are covered with a chemical called sizing. This makes the yarns strong while they are being woven.

Weft yarns go side to side. They are stretchy. Weft yarns are fed into the loom with air jets. Weft yarns cross over and under warp yarns.

AT A TEXTILE MILL

Cotton thread is woven on a loom.

For denim cloth, the warp yarns are dyed blue. Blue dye comes from the **indigo** plant. The warp yarns are dipped in a vat of indigo dye several times. This process forms several layers of blue dye on the yarn. For denim cloth, the weft yarns are left white.

Now chemicals are added to the cloth to change how the cloth looks and feels. Denim cloth can be bleached or washed with stones. It can also be sandblasted. This gives the cloth a worn look.

Levi Strauss invented blue jeans in the mid-1800s. The jeans were meant to be pants for gold miners.

The white cloth is dyed blue.

CHAPTER FIVE

At a Blue Jeans Factory

After the denim cloth has been made, it is moved on huge rolls to a blue jeans factory. There jeans are made in different sizes and styles to fit different people.

Each pair of blue jeans is made from about ten pieces of denim cloth. Patterns are cut from heavy paper. The patterns are placed on stacks of denim cloth 100 layers thick.

Workers cut the cloth through all the layers to match the pattern. They use cutting machines. These

The denim cloth is wound into large rolls.

machines look like small electric saws that move very fast.

After the pieces of denim are cut, some of the smaller pieces need to be attached to other pieces. Workers use sewing machines to sew the pieces. Each worker makes one part of the jeans. One worker makes back pockets. Another worker makes belt loops.

Then the larger parts of the jeans are sewn together. Pockets are sewn to leg seams. Leg seams are sewn together. The waistband and belt loops are attached. Buttons are sewn on. If the jeans have a

A worker cuts the denim.

Pockets are sewn onto leg pieces.

zipper, it is sewn in place. Then the pants are hemmed. **Rivets** are put in place. The maker's label is sewn on. The jeans are brushed to remove thread or lint. Then a hot steam machine blows out wrinkles. A worker punches a size tag into the label.

Workers inspect the jeans. They make sure the jeans are ready to be sold. If a worker finds a mistake, he or she fixes it. Then the jeans are folded, stacked, and placed in boxes. They are sent to a warehouse.

Rivets are added to the jeans.

CHAPTER SIX

Into Your Closet

A store orders jeans from the factory. Workers load jeans into boxes. The boxes are shipped by truck or train. You can buy blue jeans at your favorite store. You can also order them online.

Many styles of blue jeans are available. Some people like dark blue jeans. Some like jeans with a special finish. Some people like jeans that fit tightly. Others prefer loose jeans. Blue jeans can also be stretchy.

What kind of blue jeans do you like best? It is your choice! Pick some jeans and pull them on. Are you ready to play?

Jeans are delivered to the store for you to buy.

BLUE JEANS MAP

1
HARVEST COTTON

2
GIN COTTON

6
SEW PIECES

5
CUT CLOTH

32

3
MAKE CLOTH

4
DYE CLOTH

8
TO THE STORE

7
ADD ZIPPERS AND RIVETS

31

GLOSSARY

chemicals (KEM-uh-kuhlz): Chemicals are substances made using chemistry. Farmers spray chemicals on crops to keep insects away.

denim (DEN-im): Denim is a strong cotton cloth used to make jeans and other clothing. Blue jeans are made from denim cloth.

fiber (FY-bur): Fiber is a thread that forms in parts of certain plants, such as cotton. Cotton plants produce cotton fiber.

harvest (HAR-vist): To harvest is to collect crops. Different machines are used to harvest cotton.

indigo (IN-duh-goh): Indigo is a plant that has dark purple berries that are used to make dye. Indigo dye is used for blue jeans.

modules (MOJ-oolz): Modules are pressed rectangles of cotton made at a farm. Modules of cotton are taken to the cotton gin.

rivets (RIV-its): Rivets are strong metal bolts that are used on parts of jeans. Workers attach rivets to jeans at the factory.

textile mills (TEK-stile milz): Textile mills are factories where fabric is made. Some cotton fabric is shipped to textile mills.

BOOKS

Johnston, Tony. *Levi Strauss Gets a Bright Idea Or: The Positively True and Unfabricated Story of a Pair of Pants*. Boston: Houghton Mifflin Harcourt, 2011.

Masters, Nancy Robinson. *The Cotton Gin*. New York: Franklin Watts, 2006.

Morris, Neil. *Textiles*. Mankato, MN: Amicus, 2011.

INDEX

bales, 10, 14–15, 16
boll weevil, 8
carding machine, 16
cotton farm, 4, 6–11
cotton gin, 11, 12–15
denim, 4, 20, 22, 24
dye, 20
factory, 22–27
fiber, 6–7, 9–10, 13–16
harvest, 9–10
lint, 14, 16, 27
loom, 18
modules, 10–11, 12
picker, 10
seeds, 6, 8, 12–15
sliver, 16, 18
Strauss, Levi, 20
textile mill, 15, 16–21
Whitney, Eli, 12

Visit our Web site for links about blue jeans production: childsworld.com/links

Note to Parents, Teachers, and Librarians: We routinely verify our Web links to make sure they are safe and active sites. So encourage your readers to check them out!